FOCUS ON

ELECTRICITY
AND MAGNETISM

BARBARA TAYLOR

GLOUCESTER PRESS
London · Sydney

*First published in
Great Britain in 1995 by*
Watts Books
96 Leonard Street
London EC2A 4RH

ISBN 0 7496 1957 0

A CIP catalogue record for this book is
available from the British Library.

Printed in Belgium

Design	David West Children's Book Design
Designer	Edward Simkins
Series Director	Bibby Whittaker
Editor	Sarah Levete
Picture research	Brooks Krikler Picture Research
Illustrator	David Burroughs

*The author, Barbara Taylor, has a degree in
science, and has written and edited many
books for children, mainly on science
subjects.*

*The consultant, Dr Bryson Gore, is a lecturer
and lecturer's superintendent at the Royal
Institution, London.*

INTRODUCTION

Electricity and magnetism have existed since the beginning of time. They exist in many forms in the natural world around us – the Earth is like huge magnet and our bodies are full of tiny electrical signals. Over the last hundred years, we have discovered how to harness the powerful energy of electricity, together with the force of magnetism, transforming the world we live in. Today, communication, transport, industry, and leisure rely on the power generated by electricity and magnetism. This book explores the scientific principles of electricity and magnetism. It aims to provide a complete picture of how we make, send and store electricity, and how it is used, with magnetism, in our lives.

Geography
The symbol of planet Earth shows where geographical facts are examined in this book. One section looks at the environmental issues of electricity. Another looks at the different supplies of electricity around the world.

Language and literature
An open book is the sign for activities which involve language and literature. One of these sections looks at the way in which advances in technology have transformed the way in which we can read – no longer in printed books, but displayed on screen.

Science
The microscope symbol indicates where science information is included. One panel looks at how electricity is measured. Another examines the ways in which small amounts of electricity can be stored in batteries.

History
The sign of the scroll and hourglass shows where historical information is given. These sections look at key people involved in the discovery and understanding of the forces of electricity and magnetism.

Maths
A ruler and compass indicate maths information and activities. One panel considers how much electricity we use in our daily lives. Another examines how static electricity is created.

Arts, crafts and music
The symbol showing a sheet of music and art tools signals arts or crafts activities. One topic examines the way that the effects and power of electricity have been used as subjects for films. Another activity explains how to build a simple circuit.

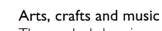

CONTENTS

WHAT IS ELECTRICITY?

Electricity is an invisible form of energy which is stored in electrons and protons. These are the tiny particles in atoms (below) which make up all matter. Electricity is created when there is an imbalance of negatively charged electrons and positively charged protons. Current electricity is made up of moving electrons which travel through wires. In static electricity the electrons remain still. Electricity is a powerful and useful source of energy, but it can also be very dangerous.

Discovering electricity

Electricity was first discovered by the ancient Greeks, about 2,000 years ago. A Greek scientist called Thales noticed that a piece of amber (the hard fossilized sap from trees) attracted straw or feathers when he rubbed it with a cloth. The word 'electricity' comes from the Greek word for amber – 'elektron'.

In 1600, William Gilbert (left), a doctor to Queen Elizabeth I of England, was the first person to use the word 'electric'. He carried out experiments and discovered that materials such as diamond, glass and wax behaved in a similar way to amber.

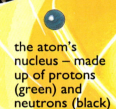

the atom's nucleus – made up of protons (green) and neutrons (black)

From the stars

The Sun and other stars send out radio waves through space. They are a form of electrical and magnetic energy which travel through space at the speed of light. They are picked up by huge dishes called radio telescopes. The radio waves are changed into electrical signals that give astronomers information about distant galaxies.

Investigating static electricity

Static electricity, used inside photocopiers and paint-spraying machines, can be generated by rubbing different materials together.

You can test materials for static charges, which are either positive or negative. Opposite charges attract things and like charges repel things. Experiment by rubbing different materials such as paper, plastic, metal, wood and rubber with a cloth. Do they attract or repel things? Make a chart of your results.

Electrons everywhere

A particle accelerator (above) is used for research into atoms. By smashing atoms together, scientists have discovered over 200 particles, even smaller than atoms. A beam of electrons in an electron microscope (above left) enlarges objects millions of times.

negatively charged electron

Switch on the light

In fluorescent lights, an electric current makes gas glow. Neon gas makes red light, sodium gas yellow light, and mercury gas makes blue light.

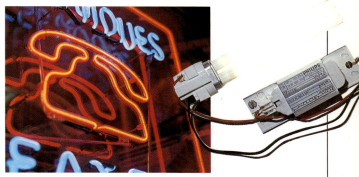

Electricity for life

Most animals rely on electrical signals which provide them with information about their environment and control the way their body works. A network of nerve cells collects the information and sends out instructions. Invertebrates such as an octopus (right) have simple nerve nets.

Humans have more complex systems. The brain has an intricate network of nervous tissue (below). Our brain buzzes with tiny electrical signals, which trigger our heartbeats, to make our muscles move and sustain our body processes.

WHAT IS MAGNETISM?

Magnetism is an invisible natural force given off by some pieces of metal or stone which have the power to attract or repel certain materials. Magnets occur naturally in rocks in the ground, but they can also be made from substances such as iron or nickel. Magnets attract iron, nickel, cobalt and most types of steel, but do not attract copper, aluminium, brass, gold, silver or lead. Some magnets are 'permanent' magnets, because they only lose their magnetic power if they are dropped or become too hot. Every day we use magnets in televisions, computers and telephones. Huge magnets help to generate electricity in power stations.

Discovering magnets

About 2,000 years ago, near Magnesia, in modern-day Turkey, from where magnets take their name, people discovered rocks in the ground which were natural magnets. About 1,000 years ago, the Chinese noticed that certain rocks always pointed north and south when they were hung from a thread. They used these magnetic rocks as simple compasses to help them find their way around the oceans. The rocks were called 'leading stones', or lodestones, because they led sailors along the right route.

Working together

Some materials can be made to act like magnets when an electric current is passed through them. These are electromagnets. Electricity flowing through a coil of wire, wrapped around a metal core, produces a magnetic field. Electromagnets are not permanent magnets; when the flow of electricity is switched off, the magnetic field disappears. Electromagnets on cranes (right) pick up heavy scrap iron. When the electricity is switched off, the iron falls off.

The magnetic poles

The Earth is like a giant magnet with a magnetic north pole and a magnetic south pole. The Earth's magnetic field is strongest at these poles, which are in a different position from the Earth's geographic poles. The magnetic north pole (near Ellef Ringes Island in northern Canada) was first discovered by James Clark Ross (left) in 1831. The magnetic south pole was discovered off the coast of Wilkes Land in Antarctica in 1909, after one of the most outstanding sledge journeys of all time. Members of Ernest Shackleton's (right) first expedition to Antarctica, David, Mawson and Mackay, survived 122 days with rations for only 93 days. The expedition covered 2028 km (1214 miles) of unexplored territory on foot, pulling their sledges behind them.

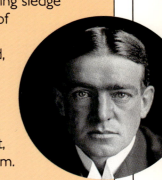

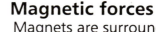

Magnetic forces

Magnets are surrounded by an invisible force – a magnetic field – which attracts things within its field. Sprinkle iron filings around a magnet. More filings cluster together where the field is strongest, at the magnetic poles (far left). Like poles repel; unlike poles attract (left). Magnets only attract each other if their opposite poles are close.

Magnetic information

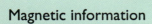

Today magnets are used in increasingly sophisticated ways. They can now 'store' large amounts of information. Computer discs hold information as magnetic patterns. A magnetic strip on a credit card identifies the holder of the card. Smart cards have this strip but they contain microchips as well, so they can be used as bus tickets, or to pay bills over the telephone, and they can even 'hold' people's medical records.

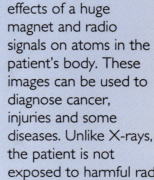

Seeing inside the body

Doctors use a technique called magnetic resonance imaging (MRI) to give them detailed 3D images of structures inside the body. The image is created by a computer from the effects of a huge magnet and radio signals on atoms in the patient's body. These images can be used to diagnose cancer, injuries and some diseases. Unlike X-rays, the patient is not exposed to harmful radiation. The technique also allows doctors to identify problems without having to operate.

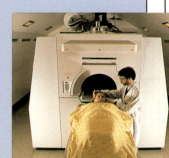

PLANET EARTH

There are many natural sources of electricity and magnetism on Planet Earth which have existed since the beginning of time. In Greek mythology, lightning, which is a form of static electricity, was used by gods such as Zeus (above) to impose authority on mortals. A magnetic field called the magnetosphere surrounds the Earth, stretching over 60,000 kilometres (36,000 miles) into space. The Earth's magnetic poles move a few centimetres each year – over millions of years, their positions have even reversed direction!

Finding your way
A compass needle is a tiny magnet, which always points to the Earth's magnetic poles. A map does not tell you which direction you are travelling in, but with the help of a compass, you can find your way. To use a compass with a map, place the compass on top of the map. Turn the map around until the north arrow on the map points in the same direction as the compass needle.

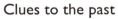

Magnetic Earth
Scientists believe that the Earth's magnetic field is produced by the molten iron core at the centre of the Earth. This metal core has melted because of the very high temperatures there. As the Earth rotates (below), electric currents are created in the core. This produces the magnetic field. Scientists believe this works in a way similar to producing electricity in a power station (see pages 14 - 15).

lines of force which make up the Earth's magnetic field

Clues to the past
Over millions of years, hot liquid rock rising and sinking beneath the Earth's continents has caused them to drift about the Earth's surface. This liquid rock has broken through the surface along ridges in the middle of the ocean floor. As the liquid cools down, magnetic material in the rock lines up with the Earth's magnetic field. The rocks have set in opposite directions, providing evidence that over time the Earth's magnetic field has changed direction (right).

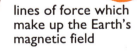

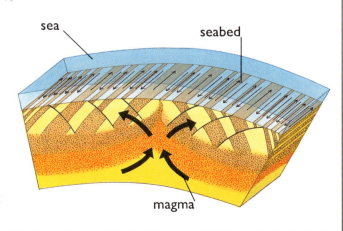

sea

seabed

magma

Electric fishes

About 500 species of fish produce an electric field from special muscles with columns of wafer-like cells, which are a bit like tiny living batteries (see pages 18-19). Species such as the elephant nose fish give off almost continuous electric charges to help them navigate and

communicate. Electric eels, rays (left) and catfish have large electric organs which can give off powerful bursts of electricity, enough to stun a person or kill a small fish. Sharks (right) pick up electrical signals from the muscles of fish. They can home in on their prey with deadly accuracy.

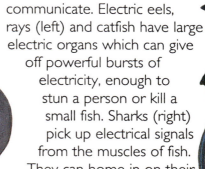

Electricity in the sky

Lightning is a huge spark of static electricity. It builds up inside storm clouds when small drops of water and ice rub against each other. Storm clouds build up either positive or negative charges as their particles are rubbed in different ways. When negative and positive clouds get near each other, giant sparks jump between them. These can leap to the ground, producing a flash of lightning. An American inventor called Benjamin Franklin (1706-1790, right) showed that a bolt of lightning was really a

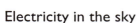

spark of electricity. In 1752, he flew a kite during a storm. Lightning flowed down the kite string, making a small spark on a metal key at the bottom of the string. This dangerous experiment led to the invention of lightning conductors – metal strips running from the top of a building to the ground. If lightning strikes the building, they carry the electricity safely to the ground. The top of a conductor (left) can be bent by the lightning's heat.

Animal migration

Many animals make long migratory journeys to find food or to avoid bad weather. They can sense the Earth's magnetic field which helps keep them on the right course. In Australia, compass termites protect their nests from the Sun's heat by building them facing north to south.

Force fields in space

Other planets in our solar system also have magnetic fields. Space probes sent out from planet Earth have discovered magnetic fields around the planets of Mercury, Jupiter, Saturn and Uranus.

The magnetic fields around Jupiter (left) are about 4,000 times greater than those around the Earth. These huge magnetic fields trap clouds of particles.

ON THE MOVE

Electricity is very useful to us because it can flow along wires to where it is needed, like water flowing along a pipe. This controlled flow of electric charge is called an electric current. A current can only flow if it is pushed along by a battery or by the force from a power station. The force which pushes electricity through wires is the voltage. The current is itself made up of billions of electrons. An electric current has to travel in an unbroken line, called a circuit. Different materials allow the flow of electric current through at different rates. This is called electrical resistance.

Giving their names

Electricity is measured in units which are named after the scientists who carried out experiments on electricity. Electric current is measured with an ammeter (left) in units called amperes or amps. The French physicist André Marie Ampère (1775-1836) was the first person to work out the mathematical values of electric currents.

An Italian physicist, Count Alessandro Volta (1775-1827), invented the first battery (page 18), the 'voltaic pile' (right). This consisted of a pile of zinc and silver or copper discs separated by pads moistened with a weak acid solution. The volt, a unit of electrical measurement, is named after him.

The Scottish engineer James Watt (1736-1819, right) gave his name to the watt, a unit of power. The German physicist George Ohm (1789-1854) worked out how to measure resistance – in units called ohms.

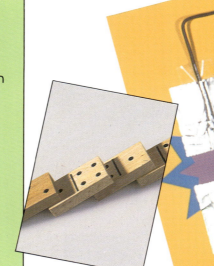

paper clip switch

Dominoes

Individual electrons do not flow through a circuit from one end to the other. They pass on their electric charge by jumping across from one atom to another. In the same way, if you push a domino over, the one at the end of the row will eventually fall down. Each domino bumps into the next one until the whole line falls down.

Conductors and insulators

In some materials, such as metals, the electrons are free to move, allowing electricity to flow through them easily. These materials are called conductors. Other materials, such as most plastics, have electrons held tightly in their atoms, so they do not conduct electricity well. These are called insulators. Metal wires which conduct electricity are insulated with rubber or plastic to make them safe.

Build your own circuit

To make a simple circuit, join a wire to each side of a bulb holder. Screw in the bulb. Join one wire to the negative terminal of a battery and the other to the positive terminal. When the circuit is complete, the bulb will light up. Make a gap in the circuit to act as a switch (right). Push two paper fasteners through a card. Insert a steel paper clip under one fastener so it can slide over to touch the other. The paper clip acts as the switch. This is an open circuit.

battery

bulb

Measuring electricity

Electric current is measured in amps. One amp is 6 million million million electrons flowing past a point in a wire each second. The electric push of a current is measured in volts. The power of electricity depends on how much current is flowing and how hard it is being pushed. The faster and harder the push, the greater the power, measured in watts. This is calculated by multiplying volts by amps. Dividing the push by current gives ohms, the resistance of a circuit – how easy or hard it is for the current to flow through it.

Stopping at the lights

A gap in the circuit prevents the flow of electric current. A switch makes a gap in a circuit so we can turn electricity on and off to control the flow or current. This process is like the action of traffic lights. When the lights are green, the traffic flows. When they turn red, the traffic stops.

Holding back the flow

The flow of electric current through a wire depends on the wire's material, length and thickness. Electric charges flow more freely through thick wires than thin ones. A thin wire (above right) has high resistance, reducing the current's flow. A thick wire (below right) has lower resistance. It increases the flow. It is a better conductor.

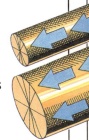

Resistance makes a light bulb work. (left). The wire filament inside the bulb is very thin. The electricity has to push hard to get through, making the filament so hot it glows white hot, giving out light. The wire is made of a metal (often tungsten) that can get very hot without melting.

Resistors are used in volume controls on televisions (right). When you turn up the volume, less wire is included in the circuit. More current flows around the shorter wire, making the sound of the television louder.

A matter of death

Electricity can be dangerous. People often get electric shocks or even die, due to accidents with electricity. Take great care with mains electricity. Make sure you do not touch anything electrical with wet hands – water conducts electricity well and may give you a serious electric shock. Some countries still use the electric chair (right) to electrocute criminals.

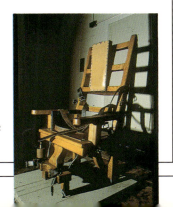

ELECTRICITY & MAGNETS

Electricity is used to make a magnetic field, and magnetism is used to produce electricity. In magnetic materials, the atoms are magnetic. These groups of atoms (domains) point in one direction (above). In non-magnetic materials, they point in different directions. Their magnetic fields cancel each other. An electric current passing through non-magnetic materials makes the domains point in one direction, creating a magnetic field. The material is magnetic as long as the electrical current flows.

coil

magnet

brushes

Making the connection
A Danish scientist, Hans Christian Oersted (1777-1857, left), first made the connection between electricity and magnetism. He discovered that a compass needle moved when electricity flowed through a nearby wire. The wire's electric current was producing magnetism, which made the compass needle move. Many everyday gadgets use magnetism which has been generated by electricity.

Electric motors make the industrial and domestic world go round. Whether in a watch, hairdryer, train or drill, the electric motor changes electrical energy into mechanical power. The diagram (right) explains how the different parts of a motor (above) work.

brushes

battery

In 1831 an English scientist, called Michael Faraday (1791-1867, below) thought "If electricity can set up a magnetic field, a magnet should be able to make an electric current." He discovered that moving a magnet near a wire made electricity flow through the wire. He invented the dynamo, a machine which produces electricity from magnetism and movement. Many bicycles use a dynamo to power their lamps. The pedalling and turning of the wheels are used to turn a magnet within a coil of wire, producing an electric current.

Electromagnets in medicine
If someone has a splinter in their eye which contains a magnetic material, surgeons can now use an electromagnet to remove it. This method is very safe because the powerful magnetic force pulls the splinter straight out from the eye. This micro machine robot (right) is designed specifically to perform such delicate surgery on eyes.

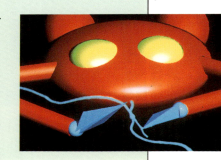

Separating metals

Electromagnets are used to sort metals in scrap yards or to separate steel cans from aluminium ones (right). When switched on, the electromagnet is a powerful magnet which picks up heavy magnetic materials. Most metals, including aluminium, are not magnetic. Once the scrap metal or cans have been sorted, they can be sent to a factory to be recycled.

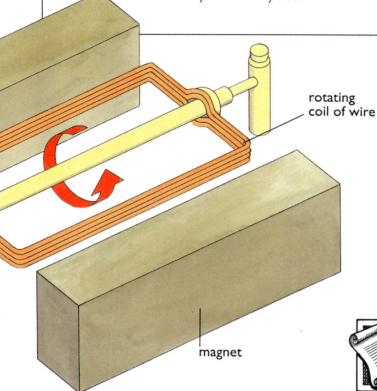

rotating coil of wire

magnet

How it works

In an electric motor, a magnet is placed around a coil of wire to create an electromagnet (see page 6) which makes the coil move. A battery is connected to the coil. The current flows up one side of the coil and pushes the other side up. This movement is repeated so that the coil spins round between the magnets. Sliding contacts – brushes – touch the end of the spinning coil so the electric current can pass in and out of the spinning electromagnet.

First attempts

In the 1870s, the German company Siemens developed the first trains pulled by electric motors. A small-scale electric railway was demonstrated at the Berlin Trade Exhibition in 1879. The train picked up power from a rail laid down the middle of the track. Although electric trains did not catch on at the time, we now use them extensively, such as the tram (below).

Words and sayings

The words electricity and magnetism are often used in familiar sayings to convey different meanings and moods. For instance if you say "the atmosphere was electric" it means that it was an exciting, charged atmosphere, when anything could happen. "To electrify an audience" means to startle or excite, as if the people had been given an electric shock. If people are said to have "a magnetic personality", they ooze personal charm and attract people to them. Can you think of any other sayings like these?

MAKING ELECTRICITY

Most of the electricity we use today comes from power stations (left). A huge dynamo called a generator makes electricity from the energy of movement, produced by using coal, gas, or oil or by the energy from nuclear reactions, to boil water. Inside the generator, an electromagnet turns inside a coil of wire, producing electricity in the coil. The current flows first in one direction and then the other. This is called an alternating current, or A.C. for short. A direct current (D.C.) only flows in one direction.

The first generators
Electricity was only available on a large scale when efficient generators such as steam turbines were developed in the 1860s. At first, these were small units which generated electricity at places where it was needed. Big power stations which supplied electricity over wide areas were not built until the late 19th century.

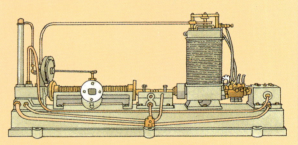

In the late 1800s the British engineer Charles Parsons (1854-1931, below) designed a quieter and more efficient turbine driven by high-pressure steam (above). The turbine blades, on the same shaft as the dynamo, made it spin at high speed to produce electricity.

Parsons' invention was taken up by the new electricity industry. The first large steam turbines were installed in a German power station in 1901.

Most modern power stations burn fuels such as coal (above), oil or gas to release the energy needed to make electricity. These are called fossil fuels because they are made from the remains of ancient animals and plants that have been preserved as fossils.

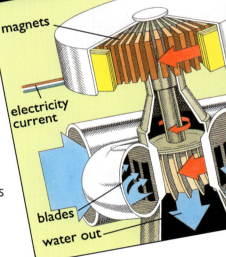

generator

magnets

electricity current

blades

water out

How a turbine works
Water-driven turbines (above) are used to generate electricity, known as hydro-electricity. A water turbine consists of fine-bladed fans running inside a tight-fitting case. Water is fed into the turbine at such a high pressure that it forces itself past the successive rows of fans, driving them round. The movement of the water turns the turbine. All the fans are connected to a single shaft which runs directly to a generator.

Fuel cells

A fuel cell converts chemical energy directly to electrical energy. Inside the fuel cell, hydrogen and oxygen combine to make electricity and water. Fuel cells (below) are silent, clean and efficient. There are no moving parts to wear out. Fuel cells are now being tried out as the power source for some buses.

In a hydro-electric power (HEP) station (above), flowing water is used to turn the turbines. Most HEP comes from big dams built across large rivers. The water falls from the top of the dam to the bottom. The water pressure drives the turbines which drive the generators to produce electricity.

Electricity and the environment

Power stations that burn coal or oil releases a lot of a gas called carbon dioxide into the air, polluting the air. Carbon dioxide builds up, forming a blanket that traps heat given off by the Earth. This causes the Earth to warm up – the greenhouse effect (below) – and causes global warming.

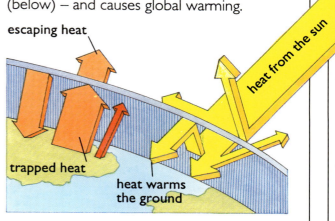

escaping heat

heat from the sun

trapped heat

heat warms the ground

Power stations discharge a gas called sulphur dioxide. This mixes with water in the air to form sulphuric acid, making rain acidic. Acid rain can kill wildlife and flora. Its acidity eats into building stone, causing it to crumble, as in this statue in Wells Cathedral in Britain.

Electricity from rubbish

A few power stations burn rubbish to turn water into steam, which is then used to generate electricity. At Wolverhampton in Britain, a power station (right) has been built to use the energy from burning tyres. More power stations like this would conserve other fuels, such as coal or oil, which are rapidly running out.

The Sun

The Sun could provide an endless supply of energy, but this is expensive to channel. In the Solar One power station in California in the United States (below), nearly 2,000 mirrors are used to reflect light on to a central tower, heating the oil inside. This can turn water into steam which is then used to generate electricity.

SENDING ELECTRICITY

Power stations send electricity through thick cables. These are usually carried high above the ground by tall metal towers called pylons. In towns and cities, the cables are buried below ground, though this system is more expensive to install and maintain. The power flows through the cables at up to half a million volts (to reduce power loss). The voltage is then lowered by transformers at substations, to a level which can be used safely in homes and offices (above). A modern mains circuit in a house carries between 110-240 volts.

A.C. or D.C.?

In 1888, Croatian-born American inventor Nikola Tesla (1856-1943) patented a system of generating and distributing electricity using alternating current.

The main advantage of A.C. over D.C. is that the voltage can easily be changed by a transformer. Tesla's induction motor (below) is still widely used as a type of electric motor.

Transforming power

Transformers at a power station (above left) increase the voltage to about 225,000 –400,000 volts. This reduces the resistance from the cables when the electricity is sent over long distances (see page 11). A transformer consists of two linked electromagnets, with a different number of turns in the coils around each electromagnet.

Electricity for all?

Today, in the developed world, people take an electricity supply for granted. Electricity has transformed domestic and working life (far right). But most of the electrical inventions we use today only date back about 70 to 100 years. Electric lights only became widely available in the 1930s. Up until the 1950s, a

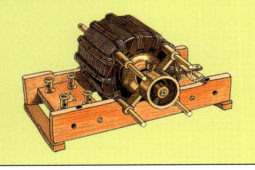

television set (below) was a rarity. With the development of electric motors in the 1930s, electrical appliances, such as small heaters and food mixers, appeared. But they were only owned by the wealthy, who made servants operate them because they were dangerous!

How much electricity?

Make a chart of how much electricity you use in one day. Start from the moment you wake up. What about the alarm clock? Your radio? How do you make your breakfast? What about brushing your teeth or running the tap? Does the weather make a difference? Will it help if you look through the TV listings?

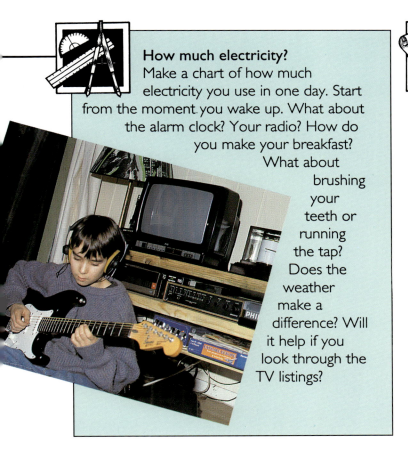

The grid

A system of pylons and cables (above left) may connect all the power stations in a country into one huge network called a grid. Therefore, if one power station breaks down, interrupting the electricity supply, electricity from another power station in the grid can be sent to replace it. This helps to avoid power cuts. The grid can also be international, with countries linked by cables capable of transmitting electricity, even across the sea.

In developing countries, one television is often shared by a whole village (right). Electric lights may be used for a short time relying on small, local generators. Power can also created by burning animal waste.

Switch on the light

Before 1900, electric lights were mostly arc lamps, where an electric spark jumped across a small gap between the ends of two rods. Then the American inventor Thomas Edison (1847-1931, left) and the English chemist Joseph Swan (1828-1914) invented light bulbs. These were cheaper, more reliable and less glaring than arc lamps. Edison tested all sorts of materials, even bamboo stems, but his first bulb used a cotton filament. It glowed for about 13 hours. Modern bulbs last about 1,000 hours. Special long-life light bulbs can last 8 times longer, using the same amount of electricity.

Power on the move

Countries can trade in electrical power. If a country has a surplus of electricity, it exports this to another country. In the spring, as the snows melt on the mountains and the rivers flow faster, Switzerland generates enough hydro-electric power to export some (below). But in autumn and winter, when the water is frozen, it needs to import electricity from neighbouring countries.

STORING ELECTRICITY

Storing electricity efficiently is a problem that has yet to be solved by scientists. Small amounts can be stored in batteries and capacitors, such as those found in electrical appliances like radios and washing machines. But it is extremely difficult to store large amounts of electricity in this way. With more and more cities being polluted by exhaust fumes from combustion engines, an efficient, pollution-free battery becomes a global necessity.

Giant sparks

In the 1930s, an American scientist, Robert Van de Graaff (1901-1967), developed a machine to collect and store huge amounts of static electric charge. A continuous moving belt passes charged brushes and transfers electricity to a storing device at the top of the machine. This transfers it to the outside of a large metal sphere, which is insulated by the column below. A Van de Graaff generator (left) can produce up to an incredible 20 million volts!

Dinorwig, Wales

In Europe's largest pumped storage station (above), water is pumped uphill at times when demand for electricity is low. When demand is higher, the water is allowed to run down again to generate electricity.

The first batteries

In 1780, an Italian scientist, Luigi Galvani, discovered that dead frogs' legs twitched when touched with a metal scalpel and pegged to iron railings with brass pins. He thought the legs must be making electricity. Volta (right) believed that the

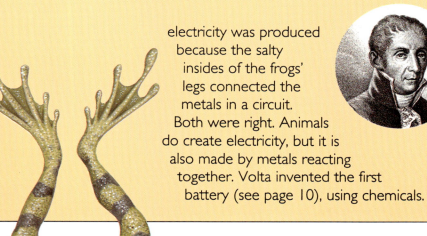

electricity was produced because the salty insides of the frogs' legs connected the metals in a circuit. Both were right. Animals do create electricity, but it is also made by metals reacting together. Volta invented the first battery (see page 10), using chemicals.

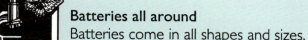

Batteries all around

Batteries come in all shapes and sizes, from the tiny round batteries inside watches, to the cylindrical or square batteries in toys or torches or the heavy batteries in cars or other vehicles. But all batteries work in the same way, storing chemical energy and changing it into electrical energy. Batteries have a much lower pushing power than mains electricity, so they are not so dangerous. Batteries can also be carried from place to place. When the chemicals inside many batteries are used up, the batteries no longer work. It is dangerous to keep 'flat' batteries because the chemicals may leak and cause damage.

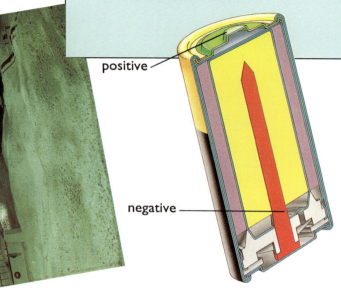

positive

negative

How a battery works

Chemical reactions inside the battery (above) build up negative charges at one terminal and positive charges at the other. This is why battery terminals are identified by plus and minus signs. When the battery terminals are joined in a circuit by a metal wire, a path is made from one terminal to the other. The electrons flow through the wire from the negative terminal to the positive.

During the 1860s, George Leclanché (1838-1882) developed a battery which did not use dangerous acids.

   The dry cell batteries we use today – in torch batteries for instance – are based on the Leclanché model (left).

Capacitors at work

In a capacitor two plates are separated by a small distance, capable of storing small amounts held in place by electrical forces. Variable capacitors (below) in radios allow you to change stations. Turning the knob on a radio changes the capacitance (the ability to store charge), causing the radio to pick up signals of a different frequency.

the amount of energy stored can be changed

Lemons into batteries

Make a simple battery from a lemon, two pieces of metal and two wires! Stick the metal pieces into the lemon, making sure they do not touch. Connect a piece of wire to each piece. Put the wires on your tongue and you will feel a tingle. Your tongue is conducting electricity produced in the lemon. A chemical reaction takes place between the pieces of metal and the juice inside the lemon. This makes electricity in a similar way to a battery.

ELECTRICITY AT WORK

Without the power generated by electricity and magnetism, the industrial world would grind to a halt. Mass production of consumer goods relies on milling machines, drills and lathes to produce parts for products which can be welded together. They are assembled on conveyor belts and lifted in loads by cranes. From metalworking to mining, the electric motor provides power which can be controlled with precision and safety. Agriculture, medicine and office work have been revolutionised by sophisticated electronic devices.

Life or death?
Hospitals in war zones (below) or disaster areas have to make do with unreliable supplies of electricity. Without advanced electrical life-saving equipment, or even basic lighting, doctors and nurses have to continue operating on the sick and wounded.

Electrolysis
In a battery, chemicals react to produce an electric current. But an electric current can also be used to cause chemical reactions, splitting chemicals into the substances they are made of. This is called electrolysis. It is used to purify metals such as aluminium (above). This is an important metal found in a rock called bauxite. Electrolysis allows us to extract the pure metal from the bauxite.

Hotting up
In electric arc welding, intense heat is created by a strong electric current leaping across a gap between two conductors (see page 10). Pieces of metal melt in order to join together. A robot arc welding machine (below) is able to work with great precision.

Electricity and farming
Electrical power and electrical machinery play an important part in the lives of farmers, their crops and their animals. Electric machines help with work such as milking cows, drying grain after harvest and moving heavy loads. Computers control the amount of food, heat and fresh air many animals receive. Electricity has also made the growing season much longer for greenhouse crops. It is now possible to create ideal growing conditions, no matter what the weather is like outside. Electric clocks control the artificial lighting to change daylength and so influence flowering times.

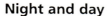

Up or down?
Escalators and lifts (left) are both lifting machines powered by electric motors. In an escalator, the motor powers a drive wheel which moves a chain connected to the stairs. In a lift, the motor drives a pulley which raises or lowers the lift by means of cables attached to the lift car.

Night and day
Industry never sleeps. This oil refinery (below) continues to work through the night, powered by constant supplies of electricity.

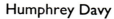

Humphrey Davy
The English chemist Humphrey Davy (1778 -1829) and his assistant Michael Faraday (see page 12) were among the first scientists to use electrolysis. Using this technique, they discovered many new elements, such as pure potassium, sodium and calcium. To make pure potassium, a silvery metal, Davy passed a current through potash, which is found in the ashes of burned plants.

Electroplating
Electrolysis is also used to give a thin metal coating to another piece of metal. This is called electroplating. If the metal is to be coated with silver, it is attached to the negative terminal of an electricity supply and dipped in a liquid containing positive silver particles. When the current flows, the silver moves to the negative terminal and coats the metal. Tin cans are made by electroplating tin on to steel.

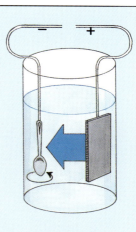

Electric mist sprays give moisture to plants and electric soil warming and irrigation encourage good root growth. Young chicks grow quickly in the carefully controlled warmth of an electronically heated incubation room (below).

Electricity in films
In the silent film *Modern Times* (1936, right), Charlie Chaplin explored the extent to which electrical machinery has taken over our lives. In the film, Chaplin's lovable character of the little tramp with the funny walk struggled to cope with different machinery. Electricity was a vital component of films about Frankenstein's monster, which was brought to life with the energy from a lightning bolt.

TRANSPORT

Without electricity, people would find it very difficult to get about, especially in the developed world. Motor vehicles use electric sparks to explode the petrol which drives their engines, and electric cars run on battery power. Across the world, electric trains (left), electric trams and trolley buses rely on electrical power, while electro-magnetic trains 'float' above the track. Diesel-electric engines pull many trains and also power many huge cargo ships and ocean liners. Aeroplanes and ships use sophisticated electronic navigation to find their way.

Car computers

Traffic computers, powered by batteries, are becoming more commonplace on car dashboards (below). They can display maps, warn of roadworks and traffic jams, plan the best route for a journey and even give the driver spoken directions. The information is received from radio beacons which feed data into a control centre.

Aircraft and ships rely on electronic navigation for direction (below). Computer-controlled equipment allows aircraft to fly on automatic pilot without manual control.

The equipment picks up signals from a chain of radio beacons on land. Satellites use this information to calculate accurately the position of the aircraft.

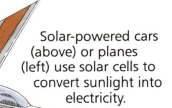

Solar-powered cars (above) or planes (left) use solar cells to convert sunlight into electricity.

Pedal power?

The Sinclair Zike (below) is an electrically powered bicycle. Batteries in the frame produce electricity to drive the Zike. The battery can be recharged and is turned on or off with a simple switch on one handlebar.

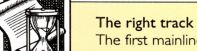

The right track
The first mainline electric trains ran on the Baltimore and Ohio railroad in the US in 1895. Electric trains take power from overhead cables or a rail next to the track. They do not need to carry fuel, but they travel near power lines. Electric track is expensive to build and maintain. Diesel-electric trains use a diesel engine to run a generator, which produces electricity to drive motors linked to the wheels. Today, trains can achieve remarkable speeds, particularly those in France and Japan.

The French Train à Grande Vitesse (TGV, right) reaches over 483 kph (290 mph) and the magnetically levitated (maglev) train has reached speeds of more than 402 km/h (241mph).

In a nuclear-powered submarine (left), an atomic reactor provides heat energy to drive turbines which generate electricity. The submarine can travel a long way without refuelling. This is an expensive source of power, and the safety of nuclear power is under question. An experimental Japanese ship, *Yamato 1*, uses electro-magnetic power to drive the ship.

Green electricity?
Pollution in cities such as Los Angeles, United States, where most people drive (below), can be a serious health hazard. However, electrically powered vehicles do not emit harmful gases into the atmosphere. But most of the electricity (except solar power) is still made in power stations that burn fuels and cause pollution. Electric cars are one step towards reducing pollution. To date, however, a satisfactory battery-powered car with good performance, has yet to be developed.

Batteries for ever
Some batteries do not need to be thrown away when they go 'flat'. Instead, they can be recharged to start up their chemical reactions again. Electric wheelchairs are run on rechargeable batteries. A car battery is also rechargeable. While the car is running, the battery builds up a store of electric current with which the engine can be restarted.

COMMUNICATION

Since the invention of the electric telegraph in the early 19th century, electricity has made it possible to talk or send information to people almost anywhere in the world. Electronic equipment converts sounds or pictures into electricity, which travels around the world at the speed of light. Telephones, faxes, televisions and radios change this back into sounds or pictures. Computers can communicate directly with each other in seconds, using electronic mail, or E-mail.

On the line

Alexander Graham Bell (1847-1922), a Scots-born scientist, invented the telephone in 1876. He realised that varying electrical signals can make a flat sheet vibrate to produce sound waves. The telephone turned them into electrical signals at one end and back into sound waves at the other end.

Radio and television

In a radio or television station, sound waves or light waves are first changed into electrical signals. A transmitter then changes the electrical signals into radio waves, which are beamed into the Earth's atmosphere by an antenna or aerial. The antennae of a radio or television set pick up radio waves from the air. The radio changes them first into electrical signals and then into the sound waves that you hear. A television set changes the radio waves into electrical signals and then into sound waves and light waves.

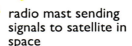

radio mast sending signals to satellite in space

Samuel Morse (1791-1872) worked out a way of sending pulses of electric current along wires to form a coded message. A code of dots, dashes and spaces represented numbers and letters. This came to be known as the Morse Code after its inventor. Morse's first permanent telegraph line opened in 1844 between Baltimore and Washington in the United States.

Satellites receive signals from relay stations, and send them to a cable station.

Satellite communication

Hundreds of communication satellites, or Comsats, are now orbiting the Earth. They receive radio signals from huge, dish-shaped aerials on the ground and beam the signals back to an aerial in another part of the world.

Picture this

Videophones (below) show telephone callers live pictures of each other while they talk. At first, they were difficult to design because moving pictures contain more information than a telephone line can carry. With digital electronics, a picture can be turned into a numbered code, to reduce the amount of information which is sent along the line.

Some television channels are transmitted by electrical signals that flow along a special cable to people's homes. This is called cable TV (left). It can transmit live reports across the world. Viewers with cable TV were able to see live international reports from the Gulf War.

From live bands (left) to high-quality recordings, music has been revolutionised by electricity. Using a numbered and shortened code, it is now possible to send compact discs (CDs, below left) of high-quality music over the phone. The Digital Compact Cassette recorder (DCC, below right) plays cassettes that have been recorded as coded numbers. The sound is of a very high quality.

Electric art

Electronic art computer programs for both drawing and painting are now becoming more sophisticated. You can reproduce different painting materials, such as oils or charcoals, smear oils together, blend watercolours and even create your own brushes by choosing the number of bristles. Paintings on a computer screen can be endlessly improved and re-touched, but it needs a lot of computer memory and a good colour printer.

THE COMPUTER AGE

Rapid advances in electronic components, such as the 'chip' (left) and computer processors, have altered our lives beyond recognition. A computer, once the size of a room, can now be tucked into a pocket. From playing games and making music to working robots, computers carry out a vast range of tasks. The Internet, an international computer network through which people can communicate, is growing so rapidly it even needs its own policing.

laptop computer

printer

modem

disc

The electronic office

Advances in computers and electronic communication have begun to revolutionise the way people work. Many people can now work from home, sending or receiving information by telephone, fax, E-mail or computer discs. This is called teleworking or telecommuting. Modems (MOdulator/DEModulator) change computer signals so they can be sent along telephone wires between computers.

Laptop or notebook computers allow people to work while travelling or in remote locations with no electricity supply.

Walking in the past

Virtual reality helps archaeologists to recreate buildings from the past and walk through them, as in the reconstruction of the Cluny monastery (right). VR may also be used in the future to link robots to humans, allowing the human to see, hear and feel everything the robot sees, hears and feels. There are plans to use virtual reality pictures in films instead of actors, for difficult and dangerous stunts.

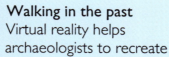

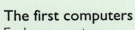

The first computers

Early computers were huge, bulky machines that used valves to control the electric current (below). In 1948 much smaller components, called transistors, were invented to control and strengthen electric current and switch current on and off. Transistors used less power than valves and were difficult to damage. In 1958 came the development of the integrated (all-in-one) circuit, also called a 'chip'. One chip can contain hundreds of thousands of tiny transistors and other components. Chips have made equipment such as computers (right) cheaper and smaller.

Is this for real?

VR computer systems create a 3D world which makes people feel as if they really are in the world made by the computer. The user wears a special helmet fitted with a visor. As the user moves the visor, sensors feed data back to the computer so the computer changes the picture. It is even possible to 'pick up' objects using a special glove that creates the illusion of gripping or lifting.

Looking it up

Electronic books store huge amounts of information on discs like those used in CD players. The disc is called a CD-ROM – Compact Disc Read Only Memory. Reflecting pits in the disc represent a code of numbers which can be read by a laser beam. This converts the data back into sounds and pictures. Once a CD-ROM is made, its contents cannot be changed, although interactive versions may be available soon.

Computers and films

The robots and computers featured in films about space and the future, such as *Star Wars* (main picture), are usually much more advanced than current models. Most of the robots look rather like humans. They walk and talk and problem-solve. They even have their own personality. In reality, most robots work in factories and do one job. They often have only one arm since it is difficult to reproduce the complex movements of the human hand electronically.

In the film *2001: A Space Odyssey* (1968), the computer, Hal (below), is a 'thinking' computer which changes its programming to ensure its own survival.

TOMORROW'S WORLD

From 'intelligent' computers and miniature robots to virtual reality (left, new developments in electricity and magnetism herald exciting advances in the future. The communications possibilities of computers, linked in global networks, open up an enormous potential for people to share ideas and information world-wide. Advances in technology have discovered new ways of generating electric power, such as that from nuclear fusion. Although these could solve some pollution problems, caused by the way we generate electricity today, there are many questions over safety.

Insect robots

As well as complex robots, scientists are also working on much simpler models which will carry out tasks by just reacting to situations instead of thinking. These 'insect' robots would be only about 30 cm (12 ins) long and weigh less than a bag of sugar. Genghis (right) is brought to 'life' by one of the researchers who helped create him. Simpler robots would be cheap and easy to build and could explore new planets before human astronauts. Closer to home, insect robots could also carry out useful tasks such as housework.

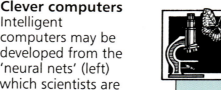

Clever computers

Intelligent computers may be developed from the 'neural nets' (left) which scientists are working on today. These computers tackle problems in a similar way to human brain cells, or neurons, which are linked in a network in the brain. Neural nets will be very important in the design of seeing and hearing systems for intelligent robots.

Fission or fusion?

At the moment, nuclear power stations split apart dangerous materials such as uranium and plutonium to release energy. This is called nuclear fission. In the future, nuclear power stations could force together safe materials such as hydrogen and helium to release the energy stored in them. This is called nuclear fusion. Fusion power would be less polluting than conventional power stations. It only needs small amounts of fuel to produce huge amounts of energy.

Global community

In the future, satellite links and vast networks of optical fibres will connect houses and businesses around the world. Optical fibres are made of glass fibres and send information as pulses of light.

Although the world powers are eager to outdo each other in their atempts to discover ways of establishing networks in space, they collaborate on projects such as the US/Russian Space Co-operation Phase (left). This co-operation extends to the use of the solar technology here on Earth, as shown above in the picture of houses using solar heating panels.

When some materials, such as tin, are cooled to very low temperatures they have no resistance to the flow of electric current. They are called super-conductors because they conduct electricity very well. They would make ideal materials for electricity cables (right) because they would waste no power, but the cooling system is expensive to run. We need to find ways of making them work at high temperatures.

Keeping track

Electronic security cameras (right) are being used increasingly to fight crime and reduce overcrowding in prisons. In some countries, people who have committed minor crimes have an electronic tag strapped to their wrist instead of going to prison.

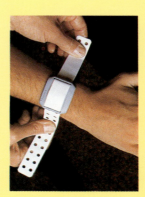

At Princeton in the United States (left), a nuclear fusion experiment produced a short burst of energy for a few seconds. The reaction took place in a Tokomak, a magnetic machine. It uses a powerful magnetic field to hold atoms of hydrogen together long enough for them to start fusing together. This is done at extreme heat.

The tag transmits a radio signal to a receiver in a person's home. If the person moves too far from the receiver, the signal becomes too weak for the receiver to detect it and it sets off an alarm.

ELECTRIC SHOCKERS

Atoms are incredibly small. A full stop or a speck of dust contains millions of millions of them.

One CD-ROM can store 100,000 pages of text, 32,000 graphic images, up to 5 and a half hours of sound, or a combination of these. A thousand paperback books will fit on to a CD-ROM.

An electric eel can store enough electrical energy in its tail to light up 12 light bulbs. A shock from an electric eel could even kill a horse.

The integrated circuits found in TVs, computers, cameras and microwave ovens contain complete electrical circuits on a silicon chip, so small it can pass through the eye of a needle.

Power stations produce hundreds of megawatts of electricity. A megawatt is a million watts – enough to light 10,000 powerful lightbulbs.

"Mr Watson, come here, I want to see you." So said Alexander Graham Bell.

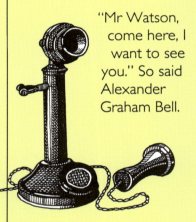

These were the first spoken words, transmitted along a telephone wire in 1896.

The electric currents in the nervous systems in our bodies travel at speeds of up to 100 metres (130 yards) a second.

The most powerful flashes of lightning contain enough energy to power a small village for a day.

The most powerful computers in the world, such as the Cray-2, can carry out up to 1,200 million calculations every second.

The amount of electricity used by a 100 watt light bulb in ten hours would be enough to drill holes with an electric drill for four hours, run a colour television for three hours or clean carpets for two hours.

Power from falling water provides about 25 per cent of the world's electricity. Some countries use water power as the main source of electricity. For instance, Norway gets 99 per cent of its energy from falling water.

Electric signals travel along wires at speeds almost as fast as light, which is the fastest thing in the universe. Electricity travels at about 300,000 kilometres (179,640 miles) per second.

GLOSSARY

Alternating current (A.C.) A current which can reverse the direction of its flow.

Amp The measurement of electrical current, measured on an ammeter.

Atom The smallest possible part of any substance. Atoms make up all matter.

Capacitor A pair of electrodes separated by a small distance, capable of storing small amounts of electricity.

Circuit The unbroken line in which an electric current travels.

Conductor A substance, such as copper, that will allow electricity to flow along it.

Direct current (D.C.) A current which flows continuously in one direction.

Domains Groups of atoms which are magnetically aligned.

Dynamo A machine which uses magnetism and movement to produce energy.

Electric charge The particles of an atom carry electric charge.

Electric current A controlled flow of electrons around a circuit.

Electric motor A machine that uses a magnet to turn electricity into movement.

Electromagnetism The relationship between electricity and magnetism – one can be used to produce the other.

Electron A tiny particle with a negative charge.

Fuse A thin wire which melts (fuses) and so breaks if the current breaks.

Grid The network of cables distributing power across the country.

Insulator A material with a high resistance, which does not conduct electricity well.

Lines of force The force of a magnet is exerted along lines of force, which extend from the north to the south pole, all around the magnet. These make up the magnetic field.

Nucleus The central part of an atom, made up of protons and neutrons.

Ohm The unit of measurement of resistance.

Pole One of the two ends of a magnet at which the magnetic forces are strongest.

Power station A place where a large amount of power is converted to electricity.

Proton A tiny particle with a positive charge.

Resistance The way in which an electrical circuit resists the flow of electric current through it.

Static electricity A non-moving electric charge often produced by creating friction.

Transformer A pair of coils on an iron core, used to change the voltage of an alternating current.

Turbine A wheel or motor driven by steam, water or air.

Volt The measurement of the electric push of a current, measured on a voltmeter.

Watt The measurement of the power of electricity.

INDEX

Photographic Credits

Abbreviations: t – top, m – middle, b – bottom, l – left, r – right.
Front cover t, m, 2t, m, 4m, 5tl, 9mr, 10t, 11bl, 12b, 13t, 14m, 15ml, 17bl, 20ml, mr, 21bl, 22t, 23ml, mr, bl, 24b 25t, m: Frank Spooner Pictures; cover b, 2b, 3t, 4t, 5tr, ml, mr, 6t, 7m all, 7bl, 8ml, mr, 10ml, mr,11t, br, 12mr, 15mr, 16t, mr, br, 17t, 18t, 19t, b, 25bl, 26m all, 27m, 29m: Roger Vlitos; 3b, 21br, 27b: Kobal Collection; 5b, 7br, 16ml, 18ml, 20b, 21t, 22mr, 26t, 28t, 28-29, 28b, 29bl, br: Science Photo Library; 6b, 12ml,: Mary Evans Picture Library; 7tl, tr, 8t, 9ml, 16bl, 18b, 24t, m, 27tl: Hulton Deutsch; 13b: Spectrum Colour Library;14t: Paul Nightingale; 15t: Ballard Power Systems; 15bl: Elm Energy & Recycling Ltd; 15br: Sandia; 17b, 22ml: Solution Pictures; 18mr: National Grid; 20t: Rover; 22bl: Gulfstream Aerospace; 22br: Whiteoaks Consultancy; 23br, 29tl: NASA; 25br: Quantel; 26b: TDI Image; 27tr: Sprekley Pittham Ltd; 29tr: A.E.R. E Harewell.